DO YOU KNOW YOU'RE BREATHING?

Simple Techniques for Teachers and Parents to Reduce Stress and Violence in the Classroom and at Home

Ruth Fishel, M.Ed., LMHC

Published By

Spirithaven

Marstons Mills, MA 02648

ISBN: 0-9660024-3-1

Published by

Spirithaven

17 Pond Meadow Drive, Marstons Mills, MA 02648
508-420-5301,
Email: spirithaven@spirithaven.com

This book is available at quantity discounts for bulk purchases

visit us on the web at
www.spirithaven.com

Dedication

To my dear son, Bob (1963-1992), who gave guidance, inspiration and joy to so many in his short life. May his memory continue to guide and inspire.

Acknowledgments

I am deeply grateful to Sandy Bierig for your patient editing and your insight and wisdom. Thank you so much for always being available, no matter what time of day, making the publication of this and all my other books possible.

Many thanks to Mary Jo Cavanugh for contributing your wise suggestions. Thank you for all your time and thoughtfulness. You are a knowledgeable and gentle teacher and your students are very lucky to be in your class.

I am so grateful for the many principals, teachers, counselors and administrators who were willing to take a chance on something new and invite me into your schools and classrooms. I especially want to mention Linda Ahern, Sue Anderson, Jane Biaggo, Jim Carey, Roy Cowling, Richard Curcio, Peg Hannigan, Beth Johnson, Edith LaBran, Sue Leary, Bruce McPherson, Mary Jane Muello, Sandria Parsons, Peg Regan, Nancy Spaulding and so many others. You will always be in my grateful heart.

A special thanks goes to high school teacher Mary Gaia who had the vision and spirit to stand up in an assembly and say, "This is exactly what we need in our school."

I am so grateful for my own teachers: Joseph Goldstein, Narayan Liebenson, Larry Rosenberg, and Sharon Salzman and the many authors who have taught me so much and have changed my life with their wisdom. It is my honor to pass on what they have so generously taught.

*We can't have peace
in our schools and in our home
until we learn to find peace
within ourselves.*

SOME RESPONSES FROM TEACHERS AND STUDENTS

Teachers have had wonderful experiences with students as they have taught STOP! In the classroom. Here are some responses from 2nd grade students when asked how they felt after practicing the ONE MINUTE BREATHING:
   Calm, relaxed, peaceful, comfortable, not as worried
   When asked what areas in their lives they could this technique:
   When I am: wild, crazy, fearful, worried
   When I am mad at my brother!
   When I can't sleep.
   When I'm punished and feel angry.

In response to the LETTING GO box, a student with ADHD reported that she liked it so much that she made one at home. "When I come to school," she said, "I can throw away home problems. Now I can throw away school problems when I get home. That way I can start fresh at both places."

Another student becomes really uptight during math tests. He said, "When my body gets all tense and I start to think "I can't do this, I focus on my breathing and it gets easier to do the math test. When it's all over I let it go so I have room in my brain for the next thing."

A teacher wrote: "Taking the time to use what I have learned during this course has helped to create a calmer, more focused atmosphere. I had used what I called "relaxation breathing" before but now I have many more strategies to use--and am calmer myself."

3rd grade students responded:
   "I feel relacsed(relaxed).
    I feel caum(calm).
    I like it because when I'm realy(really) wound up it calms me
       doun (down)."
   "I feel colm. I feel relaxed. I feel like I'm not wereing (worrying)
       any more. I feel like all my wereing thoughts are gone. It
       make me fokes (focus) on one thing, my breathing."

A 3rd grade teacher writes:
   "I used labeling(making a mental note of what it is that is
       disturbing you, IE: Noise, confusions, fear) during the State testing
       so students could tune out exterior noises. And between tests

gave them a ten minute mindfulness."
"The one minute breathing is a super way to bring them back.
(They)really tune in to the new lesson at hand."
"The walking exercise works well as the class comes back from
lunch to settle them back in."

A highschool teacher wrote:
    Dear Ruth,

       Thank you so much for taking the time to come to our
Barnstable High School English class one Wednesday morning.
The kids still talk about the benefits of trying the "de-stress"
exercise when they're feeling anxious.

Here are just a few of the many positive comments from an in-service
program for middle school and high school teachers:

"Wonderful techniques for relaxation to deal with stress."
"We can _do_ something to control the stress we and our students
feel."
"Please send Ruth to our school for staff and students."
"Repeat the workshop!"
"Extremely calming and restful learning session. Thank you,
Ruth."
"I would like her to do faculty workshops in _all_ the schools."

MCAS SPECIAL STUDY

STOP! was taught in four out of eleven 8th grade classes at the Marstons Mills Middle School in Marstons Mills, Massachusetts. The results of the tests are not in as of this writing but here are some of the students comments:

"Many times it has helped me to calm down when I have been upset. The program helped me to control my feelings without hurting myself/others."
"I felt more relaxed before the exam."
"I learned how to relieve tension throughout my body and relax."
"I found that it relaxed me and helped me to think more clearly."
"It helped me concentrate better."
"The thing I found most useful about it is how it calms you, and lets you think clearer.

Wouldn't it be wonderful?

Wouldn't it be wonderful if teachers could learn a way to feel peaceful and they couldn't do it wrong?

And wouldn't it be extra wonderful if teachers could teach it to the students and the students would feel wonderful and peaceful and the students couldn't do it wrong either?

And wouldn't it be extra, extra wonderful if the students and the teachers could each teach this to at least one other person in their families who would also feel peaceful and relaxed and they couldn't do it wrong either?

Could you just imagine what a difference this could make in our schools and our families and our towns and our cities and our states and our country and our world?

Wouldn't It Be Wonderful?

Not only is this possible, it's happening!
This book can show you how.

CONTENTS

AN INVITATION FOR PARENTS

AN INVITATION FOR PARENTS

While STOP! DO YOU KNOW YOU'RE BREATHING? is primarily written for teachers to use in the classroom, parents are teachers as well. Know that every exercise you see for school can be used in the home. Your role today at the home is at least as difficult as the teacher's role in school. However, you can find great benefit in applying these techniques to your own lives and then teaching them to your children.

May you find peace, joy and satisfaction in your role as a parent and may this book help to bring you closer to your children.

INTRODUCTION

Being a teacher is certainly not easy today. Pressure has intensified to such a degree that many of you are leaving the field you once loved so much. You began with high hopes and dreams, determined to dedicate your lives to helping students. And your job has become more and more difficult with each passing year.

Violence and alcohol and drug abuse have increased frightfully in our schools among younger and younger students. At the same time, stress is increasing alarmingly everywhere, in the home, the workplace and in the schools.

Students begin preparing now for difficult comprehensive exams as early as the first grade. By the time they are in the fourth grade, the level of stress for both teachers and students is so great that many can't perform even close to their highest levels of competence.

Family life continues to deteriorate in numerous communities. Alcoholism and drugs are common problems in many homes, regardless of socio/economic backgrounds. Single parents frequently make up a large percentage of families. When there are two parents in the home, both parents often work and sometimes do not have the time or the energy to give their children the attention and encouragement they so crucially need. In turn, many students exhibit a lack of respect and discipline for teachers, administrators and parents. The situation is becoming out of control in some schools.

In the headlines we continue to read about the increase of violence. We watch it on TV as we try to choke down our dinners. In a growing number of areas the situation is so ominous that it is necessary to use metal detectors and security guards in many schools.

There is another level of stress we haven't mentioned yet. That is the anxiety experienced by the students who are pressured to be accepted into the best colleges, pressured to get A's and B's or even only A's. Added to this, there is the pressure to join sports and clubs and groups, to be popular, to get a job, etc.

Where is all this going? Is there anything we can do?

There is a wonderful story I quoted in another of my books TIME FOR THOUGHTFULNESS:

One evening two women were walking along the beach.
Lying on the sand at the water's edge were
hundreds and hundreds of starfish. One of the women bent
down and began throwing the starfish back in the ocean.
The other woman said, "You are wasting your time. You
can never save them all."
The first woman continued throwing the starfish into the
ocean, one at a time.
"No, " she said, "But I can save this one. And this one.
And this one."

Author Unknown

And this is exactly what we can do! We can't help all of the students but we can help one student at a time.

I created STOP! DO YOU KNOW YOU'RE BREATHING? in 1985 while I was working as co-director of Serenity, Inc., a multifaceted alcoholism and drug addiction program for women which I co-founded in 1976. I taught this program to women in our halfway house and to the women who participated in SPRING, a one of a kind recovery program at MCI, Framingham, created by Sandy Bierig, the other co-founder. Changes in many of the women were so phenomenal that I began writing about the program. Eventually I published it in my book THE JOURNEY WITHIN: A Spiritual Path to Recovery. For many years I spoke around the country to therapists, psychologists, and others in the field of addiction and human services, teaching them how to bring these techniques to their clients and patients.

Then a tragedy struck my family in 1992 when my 29 year old son Bob took his life. It was totally unexpected. Bob had been an excellent student. He had been president of his fraternity and of the university inter-fraternity council. He was a big brother to many of the students, popular and respected by everyone. Bob was also a perfectionist and an over achiever.

council. He was a big brother to many of the students, popular and respected by everyone. Bob was also a perfectionist and an over achiever. One or two majors were not enough for him, he had three majors.

Upon graduation he secured a very good job in a large corporation where he became the top first year employee. Bob went on to do so well that in a few years his company offered to send him to graduate school for his MBA. They gave him a two-year leave of absence and agreed to pay for his schooling if he earned an A or B in his courses.

As a genuinely nice person, Bob had difficulty saying no to people when they asked for his help. An employee from his company called five days before exam time and Bob spent four hours on the phone helping this person, taking him away from time he needed for study. As his finals came closer, Bob panicked. Subsequently, his stress reached such a high level that he could neither sleep nor study.

Three days before finals, Bob called me in a highly agitated, fearful state. He said he couldn't study. He knew he would fail. He went on in this vein for forty-five minutes. At the end of the conversation he said, "I love you, Mom." I said "I love you, Bob." After promising to stay by my phone all day in case he wanted to talk, we hung up. I thought he was all right. That evening I received the shocking news that he had taken his life late that afternoon.

Within a few years I knew I had to bring my program to teachers and students to help others avoid being overwhelmed by the tension of performing to reach some perfect goal, and all the other stress that students are faced with in their lives.

STOP! is a very simple program. It can be used by teachers, parents, administrative staff and students alike. STOP! offers simple options and teaching tools that can be used both in and out of school, to learn life skills that can be used forever.

With my plan, STOP! is first taught to teachers for their own personal use. Then the teachers are trained to teach it to their students. Both teachers and students benefit as you will see from the feedback enclosed.

When students are taught early enough, they will know that they have options other than alcohol, drugs and violence as they get older.

THERE IS NOT ONE PERSON I KNOW WHO PRACTICES
MINDFULNESS AND WHO WANTS TO STAY CLEAN AND SOBER
WHO HAS PICKED UP A DRINK OR A DRUG AGAIN!

STOP! will give you more control in your classroom, which is essential to do your job. Applied as directed, you will see grades increase and attitudes change. The practice of mindfulness has been shown to improve grades and increase IQs.

You will find this guidebook chock full of suggestions for bringing peace and calm to yourself, your classroom and your home. The instructions are simple and easy to understand and just as easy to teach.

Practiced regularly, people will soon notice a wonderful difference in their lives. Not only will they feel increased calm, and a sense of well being, they will feel clearer about the direction and purpose of their lives.

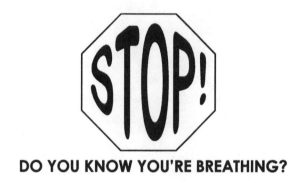

DO YOU KNOW YOU'RE BREATHING?

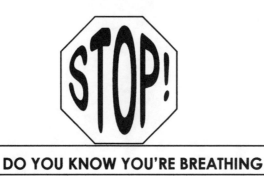

DO YOU KNOW YOU'RE BREATHING

IMPROVES THE ABILITY TO:
- Deal with tension and stress
- Concentrate, focus and learn
- Act instead of react
- Identify, label and manage feelings
- Recognize consequences of one's decisions and actions
- Identify self talk and locate sources
- Recognize the connection between ones thoughts and feelings
- Reduce the tendency to be judgmental
- Understand the perspective of others
- Develop compassion for self and others

REDUCES :
- The desire for alcohol, drugs and other addictive substances
- The inclination to look outside of ourselves to feel better
- Effects of ADD(Attention Deficit Disorder),Obsessive Compulsive Disorder, panic attacks, depression and other emotional difficulties

IMPROVES:
- Serenity, vitality and creativity
- Self-esteem and self-awareness
- Self-discipline
- Impulse Control
- Spiritual, mental and emotional condition
- Tolerance for frustration
- Insight into patterns and behaviors

PHYSICALLY HEALS AS IT:
- Lowers blood pressure and muscle tension
- Enhances immune function
- Slows down heart rate, metabolism, and respiration

DEVELOPS:
- Techniques for personal empowerment
- Self knowledge
- Develop realistic expectations about oneself
- Life skills to maintain peace within and without

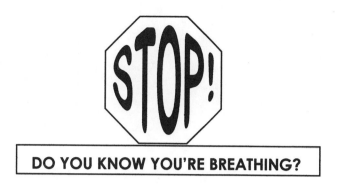

DO YOU KNOW YOU'RE BREATHING?

According to the latest medical studies people who practice mindfulness-based stress reduction regularly, report a decrease of visits to HMOs by 37%

- Heart rate, metabolism, oxygen consumption, and respiration slow down.
- Blood pressure and muscle tension are lowered.
- Along with other lifestyle changes it can lower cholesterol levels and improve the flow of blood to the heart.
- Asthma sufferers and people with chronic and acute pain find relief.
- Enhances immune function.

A BLUE CROSS BLUE SHIELD STUDY OF 2000 PEOPLE WHO PRACTICE MINDFULNESS SHOWED THEY ARE:

1. Much healthier than the American population as a whole in 17 major areas of serious disease, both mental and physical.
2. Hospitalized 87% less often than non-practitioners for heart disease and 50% less often for all kinds of tumors.
3. Equally impressive reductions in disorders of the respiratory system, the digestive tract, clinical depression, and more.

IN ANOTHER TEST researchers found that many college-age practitioners who used alcohol, cigarettes and recreational drugs spontaneously quit their habit within a few months of beginning to practice mindfulness.

Tests have also shown that with the regular practice of mindfulness, brain activity is characterized by alpha waves, which are slower in frequency, increasing mental awareness, leading to optimum functioning.

AND, PERHAPS, THE ONE WE'LL ALL LIKE BEST OF ALL:

EACH YEAR OF REGULAR MINDFULNESS IS SAID TO TAKE OFF ONE YEAR FROM THE NORMAL AGING PROCESS!

WORRY, FEAR AND STRESS

Stress is not going away, it is part of life and always will be. Stress isn't the cause of our problems. It is how we deal with it that causes us trouble. STOP! teaches new ways to deal with stress.

Worrying is a key source of stress. Thoughts such as I"m not smart enough," or "I'll never be able to memorize this," or "I have too much to do and too little time to do it," result in poor performance because they obviously take one's attention away from the task at hand. We often get caught in the worry cycle, unable to let go of these worry thoughts.

In one test reported in Anxiety Research , Bettina Seipp[1] found that: "Anxiety also sabotages academic performance of all kinds: 126 different studies of more than 36,000 people found that the more prone to worries a person is, the poorer their academic performance no matter how measured–grades on tests, grade-point average, or achievement tests."

In another study reported in *Worry Changes Decision-making: Effects of Negative Thoughts on Cognitive Processing," Richard Metzger[2]* found that "when worriers were given a fifteen-minute relaxation session–which reduced their level of worrying–before the task, they had no problems with it."

We create our own stress with our worries. We put pressure on ourselves by trying to please others, by putting goals on ourselves that we can't possibly reach, by having too many "shoulds" in our lives, and in many other ways. STOP! helps us become aware of our "shoulds" and eliminate them from our thinking.

Fear leads to more worry. Fear that we're not smart enough, fear of failure, fear that we don't have enough time, fear that we won't please the teacher or the boss, fear we won't be liked are some of the fears that keep us in a worry cycle. It is said that repetitive thoughts create grooves in our brain that keep us going over and over and around and around the same subject. STOP! teaches ways to free ourselves from those grooves.

Stress stops our ability to learn new information and access information already learned. It blocks us from being able to think rationally and intelligently.

Daniel Goleman, author of EMOTIONAL INTELLIGENCE, writes that "worry is the nub of anxiety's damaging effect on mental performance of all kinds." He tells us that worries can be stopped by changing your attention to something else.

STOP! DO YOU KNOW YOU'RE BREATHING offers a variety of techniques to help reduce stress, worry and fear.

Mindfulness is the miracle by which we master and restore ourselves.

Thich Nhat Hnah

WHAT IS MINDFULNESS?

Mindfulness is a stress-reducing breathing technique which keeps us in the present moment. It is the aware, balanced acceptance of the present moment and our experience of the present moment. It's that simple! It's opening to, or being with, what's going on in the present moment, pleasant or unpleasant, just as it is, without wanting to change it, push it away or extend it. It is simply a quieting down of our thoughts, a settling down of our minds so we can focus on the now. Mindfulness teaches us how to accept whatever is going on in the present moment.

Mindfulness is simply a quieting down of our minds and a settling down of our thoughts. When we are quiet, we become centered, we can be in touch with our creativity, intuition, that still voice inside that guides us.

Mindfulness teaches us how to get in touch with our breath, one of the most powerful and natural tools we have for stress reduction and impulse control. It is our body's natural tranquilizer. It has been scientifically proven that there is a neurological change in the chemicals of our brains when we practice mindfulness.

One source of our stress comes from regrets, resentments and attachments to the past and our projections and fears of the future. Another is how we react to what is going on in the present moment. When something happens or is said that makes us respond with anger or with fear, we become stressful.

When we are mindful, we can simply experience and accept what is happening, just as it is, whether it is welcome or unwelcome, without any judgments or wishing it to be different. Stress then leaves us and there is a wonderful peace that comes from such acceptance. With practice we learn to simply say "Oh. This is just what it is," and continue to go on with what we are doing. It deepens our concentration and intuition, expands our creativity and helps us to become more centered and emotionally balanced.

SELF-TALK

By practicing mindfulness we learn to become aware of our thoughts, the inner voices that go on in our minds, our self-talk.

Once we recognize and understand the power our thoughts have over our actions and feelings, we can learn to detach from them emotionally and observe them. We can sort out the negative and destructive ones from the positive constructive ones, and realize that we do not have to believe them. These thoughts lose their power over us because we learn to create more positive and constructive self-talk to inspire, encourage, affirm, accept, respect and love ourselves.

INSIGHT and SELF-KNOWLEDGE

The practice of mindfulness brings us self-knowledge and increases our insight. Imagine something coming up in the future that makes you nervous. Perhaps you are having an exam, a public speaking presentation or an operation. Feel how your body responds to this thought. Are you holding your breath? Does your stomach tighten or turn over? Where do you hold your fears?

Now bring your attention to a time when you felt great joy. Again, feel how your body responds to this memory. Is there a different expression on your face? Is your body more relaxed? Is your breath different? By bringing our attention to these feelings, they tend to lose their power over us. When we open up to the awareness of the present moment, and breathe into it, the feelings wash away and we can feel peace. The practice of mindfulness helps us to learn the way we respond to our thoughts and feelings.

How many times have you been driving and suddenly realized that you didn't remember driving from one place to another? How often do you find yourself in a conversation suddenly realizing that you haven't heard part of what the speaker was saying to you? Your mind has either been off in a day dream, or wondering what you are going to say next, or judging what is being said to you. Maybe it drifted away remembering something in the past or is worrying about something coming up in the future. A daily practice of mindfulness helps to develop concentration and focus. It helps to train your mind to be in the moment, to bring your full attention to what is going on in the moment. You can become more focused, have better concentration. You can become a better listener and a friend by being totally present with another person.

When we bring mindfulness into our entire lives, we also become aware of the thoughts which create our anxiety and suffering. We can see more clearly when we are holding on to anger, resentments, guilt and all other negative emotions. We learn by experiencing the feelings that are connected with our thoughts, by observing the mind/body connection.

NAMING OR LABELING

Mindfulness teaches us another powerful technique called noting. or labeling. The practice of mindfulness consists of bringing your awareness to your breath. We will discuss this in more detail later. For now, it is enough to know that your mind goes off in thoughts to take you away from your breathing. You simply become aware of what takes you away, making a mental note of it, and then return your attention to your breathing. By making this mental note, you have neither ignored it or nor struggled with it. The thought loses its hold on you and goes away.

This practice of noting can be brought into everyday life. For example, if you feel yourself getting jealous, you can simply note this feeling, and, for example, say to yourself, "I feel jealous." You will then have become an observer of your feelings. Although the feeling might still there, it loses its power over you.

WHAT DOES ALL THIS MEAN IN SCHOOL FOR YOU AND YOUR STUDENTS?

Once students have been practicing mindfulness, awareness of their thoughts grow. For example, when taking a test they might notice self-talk such as "This test is too hard," or "I'll never finish this on time." "I wish I had studied more." "I'm sure I'm going to fail." They can realize these are just thoughts and are only fears. They have the choice to sit quietly for a moment and bring their attention to their breathing. This is calming, relaxing and stress-releasing, placing them in a mental and physical state that is open to logical and clear thinking. They can then add positive thinking which releases even more positive energy. For example they can say to themselves "I have all the intelligence I need to pass this exam."

Our growing awareness of our thoughts and taking the time to name them helps to reduce anger and stress in the classroom and is a very powerful technique for impulse control as well.

My students have shared wonderful experiences beyond studying and taking tests as a result of practicing mindfulness. One boy stopped fighting with his brother. Every time his brother picked on him, he just smiled to himself, focused on his breathing and walked away.

Another student was always afraid to ride her bike down hills. One vacation some friends came over and invited her to go for a bike ride that included some big hills. Her first thought was "I can't do this," and fear filled her stomach. She was aware of her "can't" thoughts, smiled, took a few seconds to be with her breath, and said to herself, "I CAN do it!" She had a wonderful time.

WE CAN'T TEACH OTHERS UNTIL WE KNOW WHAT WE ARE TEACHING

A guidance counselor told me a wonderful story about the power of stress. Students were taking a four-day exam. It was her responsibility to collect the pencils at the end of the day and sharpen them so they would be ready for the next day. There were 250 students involved. She began to notice that about one out of every five pencils were actually broken or had bite marks on them. Soon she realized that each of the broken pencils belonged to a student from one particular teacher's class. This teacher was very nervous about the exam, far more uneasy than any of the other teachers. She had, apparently, passed her stress onto her students and they in turn either chewed or pressed down so hard on their pencils that they broke.

I know you think you're too busy! You get up too early as it is. You might have young children and therefore there is no time for yourself. Or you take care of a sick mother. Or, or, or, etc. I've heard them all!

First, know that is has been scientifically proven that

TWENTY MINUTES OF MINDFULNESS IS
EQUIVALENT TO TWO HOURS OF SLEEP!

So when you get up twenty minutes earlier to be with your breath, you will be more energized than if you had stayed in bed for an extra twenty minutes.

Second, remember, mindfulness builds your immune system, helps you to heal, expands your creativity, eases your stress, and so much more, all for giving up twenty minutes of your day.

And important to us all, it has also been said that for each year that we practice, our aging process slows down for a year!

When you say or even think that you don't have time for this, remember:

When you say
There are 1440 minutes in a day.
There are 86,400 seconds.
Mindfulness takes only twenty minutes
or 1200 seconds.
That leaves 1420 minutes or
85,200 seconds
FOR YOU!

To date, I personally have been practicing mindfulness for 21 years. When I teach the kids in school I love to tell them that because I have been practicing so many years, my aging process has really slowed down and I am actually 102 years old. Some will look at each other and then at me, not knowing whether to take me seriously. They might say "Is she really?" They're sure I'm not...but, just maybe!

Finally, we affect others by how we feel. If we are feeling peaceful and calm, those around us are more apt to take on the same mood. Therefore, it's important for you to practice what you teach! I strongly suggest taking a week to practice mindfulness for yourself before presenting it to your students. And then I hope you will continue it as an important part of your life. You will be amazed at the difference it will make in how you deal with your own stress and how you will affect others around you.

With continued practice, this new way of thinking will become automatic for you in your own life and you will be able to pass this along to your students.

*"If you can't build five minutes of quiet time
into your daily schedule, it's time to face the music:
you're losing your mind, if not your soul."
Miller*

HOW TO PRACTICE MINDFULNESS

I suggest that you practice sitting with your breath at least 20 minutes a day. Morning is the best because you can carry the awareness gained with you for the rest of the day. I like to compare it with being in a cold room with the heater not plugged into the electricity. You can plug the heater in first thing in the morning and have a warm room for the entire day. You can plug it in later and be warm only for that shorter period of time. Or, you can leave it unplugged and be cold!

By bringing your attention to your breathing the first thing in the morning, you will have this technique and all the awareness that comes with it available to you all day long! You will learn to bring your awareness to your breath, thoughts and feelings more and more often during the day. As you do it, your breath will be more available to reduce your stress and help you to stay balanced and relaxed in the present moment.

DAILY PRACTICE
•**Wear comfortable, loose clothing.**

•**Sit in the same place each day, if possible.** This place will soon have a special meaning for you and in time you will feel relaxed just passing by or when you imagining your relaxation place.

•**Sit comfortably, with your back as straight as possible**, your chin tucked down enough so that the back of your neck is straight. If you are sitting in a chair, have your feet uncrossed and flat on the floor. If you are sitting crossed-legged, it is okay to lean against the wall, if you wish, with your back as straight as possible. The only position to avoid is lying down, as that is more conducive to falling asleep! Leaning over or slouching leads to shallow breathing which can make us feel tired as it reduces oxygen intake. Sitting straight allows your breath to come in deeply. This maximizes its energizing effect.

• **You can make a tape** from the following script or order tapes listed in the back of this book to help guide you into relaxation and mindfulness. Begin here if you are taping:

Now spend a few minutes being aware of your breath as it comes in and goes out of your nose. You can also let your attention settle on your chest as it rises and falls, or your stomach as it fills and empties.

Close your eyes very gently and begin to breathe in and breathe out.

Don't try to control your breathing in any way. Just let it be natural.

Now...

Let your entire body relax.

Let your breath take on its own natural rhythm.

Feel relaxation flowing from the top of your head

all the way down to the bottom of your feet.

Feel your scalp relaxing...

your forehead...

eyelids...

all the muscles around your eyes.

Relax your nose...

sinuses...

all the bones and muscles of your face.

Relax around your jaw, where we hold a lot of tension.

Now relax your mouth...

chin...

down your throat.

Feel all your tension pouring down the back of your neck...

pouring down and over your shoulders.

All tension and stress, anxiety, resistance,

all negativity

pouring down your arms...

into your hands and fingers...

into the tips of your fingers

and completely leaving your body through the tips of your

fingers.

Now relax your chest...

diaphragm...

all the knots and muscles of your stomach.

And let any stress you still might have pour

down your spine...

all stress and tension, fear, negativity

feel it emptying down into the small of your back

down through your hips...

buttocks...

thighs...

down through your knees and legs...

into your ankles...

toes...

into the tips of your toes...

STOP! DO YOU KNOW YOU'RE BREATHING? By Ruth Fishel

and completely leaving your body through the tips of your toes.

Now go back and check your body for any left over tightness and bring relaxation to them.

And then return your attention to your breathing

as you breathe in

and you breathe out...

as you breathe in

and you breathe out.

Know that as you breathe in,

you are breathing in powerful, positive energy.

You're breathing in peace

and breathing out tension.

And as you breath out you are exhaling.

You're letting go of everything

that is keeping you from feeling peace.

Now get to know all the characteristics of your breath.

Let it be your primary focus.

Sit quietly and be aware of your breathing.

Be aware of your breath

as it goes in and as it goes out of your nose.

Just notice your breath,

as it goes in and as it goes out.

See if you can notice if it's cool or warm,

long or short.

Is it rough or smooth?

Don't change it. Just let it be and observe it as it is.

Notice if it's shallow or deep.

Notice if it changes.

If thoughts come in, just let them be and return to your breathing.

If feelings come up, just notice them and go back to your breathing.

If you experience an itch or a pain, try not to move.

Bring your attention to that area of your body and watch mentally it as it changes and moves away.

If you become lost in a thought or a daydream, just notice that you are there and bring your attention back to your breathing.

It's helpful to make a mental note of what it was that took you away from your breathing.

Name it without judgment and then return to your breathing.

Know that as you are breathing in, you are continuing to fill with powerful, healing energy.

And as you breathe out you are exhaling everything negative that blocks you from feeling good.

Breathing in peace...

Breathing out tension...

Breathing in love...

Breathing out resentments...

Breathing in...

Breathing out...

    Breathing in...

       Breathing out...

Stay as long as you wish with your breath. Twenty minutes would be good. And then, when you are ready, bring your awareness back to your room. Be sure to count to five and very slowly open your eyes.

When we practice this type of breathing, we go down to a deeper level of consciousness, from a beta state to an alpha state. Our breathing, pulse, respiration and heart beat all slow down. Therefore it is important to take this few seconds to count to five before you open your eyes so that you can gradually to normal consciousness.

WHAT YOU CAN DO IN YOUR CLASSROOM

"The greatest discovery of any generation is that human beings can alter their lives by altering their minds."
Albert Schweitzer

The following pages offer an extensive variety of exercises and techniques for you to teach to your students. Some of them will need to be modified for the appropriate age level of your class. For teachers with lower grades, you can take the essence of the ideas and put them in a framework your students can understand. Students with special needs and learning disabilities have also responded positively to STOP!

The following story is a wonderful way to introduce the power of mindfulness to your students.

Thich Nhat Hahn, a famous Buddhist Monk, teaches mindfulness all over the world to promote world peace. He was nominated for the Nobel Peace Prize by Martin Luther King for his courageous work during the Vietnam War. His story is a wonderful example of the power of mindfulness, and always makes a tremendous impression on students when I tell it to them:

Buddhists were forced to leave their homes in Vietnam because the government wouldn't let them practice their religion. Their lives threatened, thousands of terrorized people fled by piling into boats and setting off to any country that would allow them to come ashore. Thich Nhat Hahn helped many of these people find safe places to live.

On one occasion there were 800 hungry people all crammed into one boat. No country would allow it to come ashore. Thich Nhat Hahn knew that he must exhibit a peaceful presence in order to negotiate with the country's ruler and save the "boat people," as they came to be known. He took a small boat to shore, stopping to take time to be aware of his breath.

Thich Nhat Hahn vowed that if he couldn't bring peace to himself in spite of all that was going on, he would never teach mindfulness again. He was able to talk quietly and peacefully with the country's leader and persuade him to agree to allow the people on the boat to enter his country.

This experience illustrates that no matter how difficult life might be, whatever our circumstances, the practice of mindfulness makes it possible to feel peace in any moment.

Try these ideas out and see what works best for you and your class. Once you begin to introduce the concept of mindfulness, you can personalize the exercise according to your own population, and go on to create more of your own.

Not only will you find an immediate change in the climate of your classroom, but as you get used to teaching this process, you will also begin to see a positive change in your own life!

INTRODUCING STOP!

I involve the students right away by asking them what things bring them stress. I'm always amazed at how quickly they respond!

The following is a list of stressors from fourth graders:

parents	brothers	sisters	cousins
pets	marks	exams	homework
teachers	being sick	divorce	mother's boy friend
sports	being hurt	being teased	someone dying
too much to do	gossip	boredom	friends moving away
being punished	parents fighting		

WORRY, FEAR AND STRESS

It's best to begin with a simple overview of stress and how worry and fear lead to so much of our stress. You can take the information from the introduction and use any or all of it, according to the level of your students. Introduce them to the basic idea that fear and worry are two of the greatest barriers to learning, and that our breath can relieve a great deal of it.

Fear creates stress. Fear closes us down as our bodies prepare for fight or flight. We create so much of our stress in our minds which then manifests itself in our bodies.

**Our bodies do not know the difference
between something real or imagined.**

Therefore, our bodies respond to what is in our minds. For example, if we think that a tiger is going to walk in the door our bodies go into stress mode. And if a tiger is really coming in the door, our bodies go into the same stress mode.

During stress, the release of chemicals is a survival mechanism that happens automatically in response to an emergency, preparing us for fight or flight.

Our bodies:

Release adrenaline and noradrenaline

Heart rate rises

Metabolism increases

Muscles tense

Breathing becomes rapid

Anxiety, hostility and anger increase

This reaction can be triggered by:

A loud noise

Perceived or real danger

Or a fear thought (**False Evidence Appearing Real**)

Most important to understand because it influences our ability to learn and remember:

The brain decreases the production of the faster beta waves
and enhances the slower alpha, theta and delta waves.
OUR MINDS CLOSE DOWN!

Mindfulness produces the exact opposite results:

Heart rate, metabolism, oxygen consumption

and respiration decrease

Blood pressure and muscle tension are lowered

Simply bringing our awareness to our breathing can help us stop many of our fears and our stresses, and open our minds!

Here is a wonderful story to read to your students to get this point across.

A citizen was arrested and shut up in a dungeon by a ferocious jailer who carried a big key. After he was thrown into it, the door of his cell was shut with a bang. He lay in the dark dungeon for twenty years. Each day the big door would be opened with a great creaking; water and bread would be thrust in and the door would be closed again.

After twenty years the prisoner decided that he wanted to die but he didn't want to commit suicide, so the next day when the jailer came he would attack him, and the jailer would kill him. In preparation he thought he should examine the door, so he turned the handle, and to his amazement, the door opened. He found that there was no lock. He groped along the corridor and felt his way upstairs. At the top of the stairs two soldiers were chatting, and they made no attempt to stop him. He crossed the great yard. There was an armed guard on the drawbridge but he, too, paid no attention to him. The prisoner walked out a free man. He went home unmolested. All that time he had been a captive, not of stone and arms, but of false belief. He had only thought he was locked in.

ONE MINUTE BREATHING

An excellent way to introduce your students to the benefits of noticing their breath is to have them count how many times they breathe in and out in one minute. Explain to them that an in-breath and an out-breath count as one breath. Have them begin counting from the time you say "start" until the time you say "stop." Be sure you have a second hand on your watch or on a wall clock.

Explain that there are no rights or wrongs here. Each student has a different rhythm. And their breathing varies all the time. If they have been just running or they are anxious, the number of breaths in a minute will increase. If they have just been sitting quietly, and have been very calm, their breathing will be slower and they will have fewer breaths to the minute.

At the end of this minute have the students share the totals of how many breaths they took in that one minute.

The importance here is for them to become aware of what they experienced in this minute. In this one minute, most students will be able to concentrate on their breathing and counting their breaths, thus leaving behind any thoughts they might be having. They will learn how they can use this exercise any time they choose.

This is a wonderful technique to stop one's busy mind from worry, repetitive thinking, obsessive-compulsive thinking and negative thoughts. It breaks their repetitive thinking cycle, changes their focus, and brings about peace. It also helps with anger, irritability, and addictive thinking. Rather than acting out in anger or other destructive emotions, your students can spend one minute with their breath and notice the difference in how they feel. We will discuss this in greater depth at a later time.

Some questions to ask:
Did the time feel long or short?
Were you surprised?
What feelings did you notice?
    Did you feel impatient?
    Self-conscious?
    Calm?

What else?

Can you see times when you might use this in your life?

Before a test?

Doing something new?

Asking someone out for a date?

LETTING GO BOX/GARBAGE CAN

It is practical as well as fun to have a LETTING GO BOX or LETTING GO BAG in your classroom. Simply take any box or bag and label it "LETTING GO" or "WORRY BOX" or "WORRY BAG." Add any decorations you wish, using paints, crayons, glitter, and so on, making it as simple or fancy as you like. Some teachers have used a miniature desk size garbage can that they have found in a store. I know someone else who made little bird house and painted "Worrying is for the Birds" on the front. It will mean more to your students if they can participate in the planning and decorating.

When students come into the classroom at the beginning of the day they can write down anything that is disturbing them and put it in the bag or box. They can include any unpleasant or worrisome situation that is going on at home or any emotion that can give them trouble during the day such as fear, anger or sadness.

The simple act of writing it down helps to let the situation or emotion go. When the thoughts or feelings come up for them, they can remember that they have put them into the worry box or worry bag and can let it go mentally.

This is not to suggest that their personal problems are to be ignored. It is also very important for students to have a place where they can talk about the things that are bothering them and to get advice and assistance in solving their problems.

The value of this exercise is that it helps to stop needless worry and repetitive thinking. It helps to free their minds so they can be more focused and then deal with their problems at the appropriate time.

"Letting go, my hands are free to grab on to life."
Rokelle Lerner

This exercise can be followed up at the end of the school day. Students can write down the stress they are feeling from school and put that paper in the bag or box before going home. This will help them to learn to be free to be mindful of their time at home, experience where they are, without worrying about school while they're home and home when they're in school.

It is very important to assure the students that you will respect their issues and will never look at what they put into the box.

A variation of this idea to reserve a shelf for students to leave their worries when they enter the classroom. You can tell them that they can pick up their worries on their way out when the class is over!

Another suggestion is to have a second box that can be used for things that students might want you to know about, but are afraid or too shy to talk directly to you.

EXCUSE BOX

Yet another variation is the excuse box. How many times have you heard "I didn't do my homework because I was sick" or "My dog ate my homework"?

Let the students write down all their excuses and the people they blame for their lack of doing some assignment and then put the paper in the excuse box. You can make this a class project someday by having the students vote on the funniest one.

HOW DOES STOP! IMPROVE ONE'S ABILITY TO LEARN AND REMEMBER?
The File Cabinet in our Minds

Remember that worry damages our mental performance. Worry produces anxiety and stress which blocks our ability to learn, memorize and perform well on exams and homework. By practicing mindfulness daily, we can notice when worry thoughts begin and not let them go on and on, blocking information from being stored in or accessed from our memories. We can bring our attention elsewhere, whether it be to our breath, an affirmation, or looking out of the window and watching a cloud drift by.

One excellent way to have your students understand how worry thoughts stop their ability to learn is to have them imagine that their minds are like filing cabinets.

Ask them to picture this file cabinet with two open drawers. When they are relaxed, the drawers remain open, allowing new information to be stored and previously-stored information to be accessed. Explain that the doors to the file cabinet close when they are in an anxious and stressful state. For example, the doors stay shut if they are afraid they won't pass the test or be able to do their homework.

By simply bringing their focus to their breathing, the file cabinet drawers remain open. When one gets out of the worrying or thinking cycle by staying with their breath, mental and physical relaxation takes place.

By practicing mindfulness and other stress-reducing techniques, stress is released and we can now open the file cabinet. We can accumulate and save new information and retrieve stored information.

INCREASING CONCENTRATION AND FOCUS

Ancient wisdom compares an untrained mind to a monkey, swinging from branch to branch at whim, doing whatever it wants to do at any time. This is not only chaotic and out of control, but also stressful and is the breeder of all kinds of disease(dis-ease), unhappiness and loss. An untrained mind is full of reactions and projections to everything that occurs. It is based on earlier conditioning and is not really aware of what is going on in the moment. It is not in charge! This is most often experienced when we are least aware, even in the morning when we are barely awake. We might suddenly feel agitated, depressed or fearful and do not know how we got that way!

When our mind concentrates on one subject at a time, such as totally experiencing this breath coming in...this breath going out, tension leaves us. We are fully present in the task that we are doing, whether it be studying, taking an exam or simply having a conversation with a friend.

The longer we practice mindfulness, the easier it becomes to experience the moment in its fullness, free from past conditioning and reactions. We gain insight into what is really going on in the moment and learn to change what needs to be changed to bring peace into our daily lives.

EXERCISES TO BRING YOUR ATTENTION TO THIS MOMENT

Here are a few guided imageries that will take you right out of a worry cycle and instantly bring you into the present moment. They are very simple and work instantly. Try these and make up your own. Try to leave a few minutes at the end of each exercise, for the students to share their experience or ask questions.

Shoes
This one is a lot of fun and brings a smile to all ages.
Say to the students:
Relax and close your eyes very gently.
Imagine your feet in your shoes.
Now imagine your toes on your feet in your shoes.
Now imagine your toe nails on your toes on your feet in your shoes.
And now, imagine a smiling face on each toe nail on each toe on your feet in your shoes!

Hands
This awakens your senses to the present moment.
Say to the students:

Relax and close your eyes very gently.
Now place your right hand over the knuckles of your left hand.
Are the knuckles of your left hand rough or smooth under the palm of your right hand?
See if you can feel whether your left hand is warm or cool.
Can you tell whether the palm or your right hand is warm or cool?
Can you feel a tingling under the palm of you right hand coming from your knuckles?

Are you aware of any other sensations in your right or left hand?

Sky and Earth's Energy

This is great before taking an exam.

Say to the students:

Relax and close your eyes very gently. Let your entire body relax.

Feel your body where it connects with the chair.

See if you can feel your clothes where they touch your body.

Now feel your feet as they connect to the floor.

In your mind picture the ground that the building is sitting on.

Imagine there is powerful energy coming up from the ground up to the floor where you are sitting.

Imagine that you feel this powerful energy coming up from the ground to the floor to your feet.

Imagine this powerful energy pouring through your body. Feel it in all the cells of your body.

Now imagine the sky above the building.

Imagine powerful energy coming from the sky.

Imagine it coming in from the roof down to the ceiling and into your body through your head.

Imagine that powerful energy pouring through your body.

Feel it in all the cells of your body.

Know that you are alert and awake and wise.

(If used before taking an exam, add:

Know that you have all the intelligence you need to do great in this exam.)

Take as long as your want for this exercise. You can let the students sit for a few minutes feeling this energy pouring through them or you can bring them right into a mindfulness exercise and let them relax for as long as you wish.

FINGER LABYRINTH

The labyrinth is one of the oldest contemplative and transformational tools known to humankind. It differs from a maze in that it offers only one route to the center and back out again. Most labyrinths are walking labyrinths where you set one foot in front of the other.

This simple finger labyrinth can serve the same purpose, to still the mind, release stress and find balance and peace. It is also known to bring balance to our right and left brain. It is a wonderful exercise to do before an exam and takes very little time.

Photocopy enough sheets of the next page for all the students. Simple directions are on the top of the page.

Finger Labyrinth

Relax and be aware of your breath. Let your finger take you on a unique experience. Begin at the entrance and follow the path slowly with your finger or the eraser end of your pencil. Let go of all preconceived ideas and find balance, relaxation and peace.

PERSONAL POWER

Mindfulness gives us:
- the power over how we react to situations in our lives
- the power over our perceptions of the world
- the power to do what is necessary for our personal growth
- the power to create joy and satisfaction in our lives
- the power to feel good about ourselves
- the power to act
- the power to love
- the power to make positive choices

SUPPORT TIME

We all know the importance of talking about our problems. When we keep things inside, stress builds. Concentration and learning becomes difficult, if not impossible. I know you have very little time, but if at all possible, offer students a chance to talk. If this is impossible with your own schedule or you feel that it will add to your own stress level, suggest that they see the guidance counselor when you feel they are having a difficult time.

Awareness
Rests in the Breath

Calmness
Rests in Awareness

Calmness Rests in the Breath

We have the power in each moment to:
Calm down
Be positive
Let go of fear
Handle anger
Feel peaceful

THE POWER OF WORDS

Words are wonderful! They can lift your spirits, inspire you, change your mood, give you courage, make you cry, and much more. As students become aware of their self-talk, the words that they say to themselves in their minds, they can be mindful of the effect the words have in their lives. And then they can see how they can change the words to change their moods and change their lives!

Our bodies don't know the difference between something real or something imagined. Our bodies respond to what we think about as if it were real. Ask your students to see how their feelings change when they think of something that makes them smile, or feel gentle or happy such as: a puppy, a lollipop, or a sunset.

Words can block us from success or bring us success. Here are some examples you can show your students:

Negative Blockers

When I say "I can't", then I can't. I'll feel inadequate.
When I say "I'll never be able to_____",   then I never will be able to_____. I'll feel incapable.
When I say "I haven't enough time," then I'm all about not having enough time. I'll feel rushed and full of anxiety.

Positive Releasers

I AM TERRIFIC JUST THE WAY I AM!
I am feeling peace in this very moment.
I feel peace pouring through my entire body.
I have all the intelligence I need to pass this test.
Peace and relaxation flow through me with every breath I take.

We are what we think about!

What we think
about
expands.

.. *watch for miracles!*

We feel what we
think about.

We create what we think about in our lives.

When awareness increases, we draw to us
what we think about.

We attract what we think about.

THE POWER OF AFFIRMATIONS

*"Thoughts of your mind have made you what you are
and thoughts of your mind will make you what you become
from this day forward."*
Author unknown

The more we practice mindfulness, the more we are able to hear how we talk to ourselves. We increase our ability to be aware of how our thoughts affect our moods and our actions. As we learn to quiet our minds we can listen to our self-talk. We begin to see these words have the power to make us feel good or bad, confident or fearful, positive or negative. It has been scientifically proven that the words we tell ourselves can heal us or make us sick. It has also been scientifically proven that positive words increase the flow of our endorphins, our feel good hormones, thus making us feel good! Negative thoughts block our endorphins and that can lead to depression.

Once we realize that how we feel is a direct result of how we talk to ourselves, then we have a new and powerful tool to change how we feel. We have a choice. Affirmations are powerful tools to help us break away from our past messages, our automatic reactive thoughts. By changing our thinking we can change our attitude, which helps us change our actions, so we can change our lives.

Affirmations are so simple that many people think they are too simple to work. I have used them and have taught them to thousands of people and the results have been amazing.

Affirmations are positive statements we say to ourselves. Affirmations must be:

1. **POSITIVE.** Say "I am confident today," not "I am no longer negative."

2. Said and felt with **PASSION and POWER.** "I am CONFIDENT today!"

3. Kept in the **PRESENT** moment. Say, "I am confident TODAY," not "I will

be confident."

4. **POSSIBLE**. I cannot affirm that I am a famous singer as I am tone deaf; but I can affirm that I am a successful writer.

5. **PERSONAL**. We can not affirm for someone else, only ourselves.

Examples of affirmations:

   I am a terrific baseball player

   I am passing all my tests today

   My mind is relaxed and open to learning all that I need to learn today.

   I have all the time I need today to do everything I need to do that is good and right in my life.

   Whenever I have a situation I don't know how to handle, I can find peace by letting it go. I can also write it down on a piece of paper and put it in my Letting Go Bag.

   Other examples of affirmations can be found in the Positive Releasers section on The Power of Words page.

NUTS! A Fun Way to End Negative Thinking

Negative thinking is so often a part of our minds that we rarely notice anything wrong with it. We just take it for granted that that's the way we are. We let negative tapes such as "I'm not smart enough," or "I'll never pass this test," perpetuate our negativity.

It is important to know that you can only have one thought
in your mind at a time.

We can choose whether that thought is positive or negative. The more times we turn a negative thought into a positive one, we form new thinking habits. We actually form new pathways in our brains.

So, how does NUTS work? Each time you hear your self-talk being a negative barrier, yell STOP! Picture a large red stop sign with big, black letters that spell STOP!

And then say

NUTS!

This stands for

Negative and Unpleasant Thought Stopping

Now, it's difficult to picture a Stop Sign in your mind and yell STOP at yourself without smiling. It is even more difficult to say NUTS! To yourself without smiling.

So remember this little trick and pass it on to your students. It works!

GUIDED IMAGERIES

Guided imageries are excellent tools to use to help the students relax. Our bodies cannot discern the difference between real and imaged situations. Our bodies believe what our minds imagine, thereby responding to real or imagined situations in exactly the same way. For example, if we smell something burning and immediately think, "The building is on fire! I'm going to get hurt!," our bodies will believe this and immediately go into a flight mode. Adrenalin will be released and our breath, pulse and heartbeat will become more rapid. On the other hand if we smell something burning and think "Something smells strange. I'd better check out what is going on," we remain calm. Our bodies will remain relaxed because our thoughts remained calm.

What we think becomes our reality.

Visualizations are excellent tools to turn the negative tapes into positive ones. They can help one begin to move away from fearful thoughts towards thoughts of confidence and accomplishment. Athletes do this all the time by visualizing successful swings, putts, hoop shots, dives, etc. By imagining that you have already achieved new goals by creating a positive new picture in your mind and then letting your body actually experience the feelings as if it has actually happened, you will be able to create new positive experiences with more and more ease.

Visualizations are like dress rehearsals. If you imagine a situation often enough, by the time that you actually find yourself in that situation, it will be familiar to you.

Practicing with the students.

Ask your students to imagine a time when they felt very confident, a time when they were successful. Ask them to remember how that felt in their bodies. Then ask them to imagine that they are sitting at their desk and taking a test. Tell them to feel the same feelings: confident, relaxed and comfortable. Practice this a few times before taking a test. If they do this often enough they can form new habits so that their minds and bodies will respond as they choose when they're in the actual situation.

Creating a Special Place

Here is a script you can read; or make up one of your own. First instruct the students to sit in a relaxed position with their eyes closed while you read or speak to them.

There is a very special place inside each and every one of us. It's a place where we feel perfectly safe, a place where we can find peace. In your mind design a perfect place for yourself. It can be anywhere at all, near the ocean or the mountains, or the forest, or the desert, or anywhere at all. It can be a place where you have already been or a brand new place in your imagination. Create a place in your imagination where you feel absolutely safe and really good about yourself. This is your special place. No one else can go there unless you invite them. It's a place where you can be peaceful and relaxed.

Now be aware of your breath as it comes in and goes out.

Let yourself see your special place. Imagine you are walking to it now. Take some time to use all your senses to know your special place. Do you hear any special sounds? Smell any special aromas? How does the ground feel beneath your feet? What time of year is it? What time of day?

Imagine you have everything you need here...everything you want.

Create a place of comfort and relaxation.

Every time you breathe in, feel yourself filling with peace and as you breathe out, your are breathing out tension and anxiety.

Feel peace flowing through your entire body. Spend some time letting yourself feel really good about yourself.

Now, imagine taking your exam in this special place where you feel relaxed and confident.

You can say positive words to yourself here such as:

> I am a good student.
>
> I am passing all my exams with ease and confidence.
>
> I have all the intelligence I need to do well on my exam today.

You can build confidence and self-esteem while in this special place by saying to yourself:

> I am terrific just the way I am.
>
> I am likable and fun to be with.

You can imagine yourself doing well in sports or other activities such as speaking before the class or applying for a job.

Know this is your special place, where you can always come to be alone and find solitude, where you can find peace and inspiration.

Stay here as long as you wish and whenever you are ready, count to five before you open your eyes.

LETTING GO BAG

Here is a script you can read to the students to help them let go of tension or any problems:

Sit in a relaxed position and close your eyes very gently.

Begin by taking a few minutes to be with your breath, breathing in peace, breathing out tension. When you feel calm and relaxed, imagine that you're in your special place.

In your mind create a beautiful bag. It can be made out of any material you wish. Design it any color, size or shape. Write the words Letting Go" or any word or phrase that feels comfortable to you on it.

Now add two handles to the bag.

Now think about a problem you haven't been able to solve or a situation about which you are unhappy or uncomfortable. Imagine that you have a pencil and piece of paper in your special place. Imagine yourself writing this down. Then, fold the paper and put it into your Letting Go Bag.

In your mind see yourself step outside your special place, taking your Bag with you. Look up and see a magnificent hot air balloon hovering above you.

Imagine it in any color and design that appeals to you.

There is a string hanging from the balloon. Tie the string to the handles of your Letting Go Bag and feel yourself letting go of it!

Watch the balloon begin to rise, going higher and higher, up in the sky. See it becoming smaller and smaller until you can barely see it at all.

Let yourself feel lighter! Know that the balloon has taken your special problem or situation and all the energies of the universe are now working on it for you. You will know what to do when the time is right.

There's nothing else you have to do. Every time this situation comes up for you, just let it go, know that you have done all you can do at the moment.

Take some time to feel the peace and comfort of letting go.

And when you are ready, come back to your room.

Be sure to count to five before you open your eyes.

LETTING GO VISUALIZATION

Sometimes thoughts get locked into our brain and it seems as if we can't let them go. They might go away for a little while, but they keep on coming back when we least expect them. This exercise helps you to let go of thoughts or put them aside for another time, a time when you choose to think about them. This puts you in charge of your thoughts, not your thoughts in charge of you!

Can you think of an example of something you think about but don't want to think about?

Think about something that is concerning you, that keeps you from being in the moment.

Some of the things are important, such as perhaps getting a job, or thinking about the exam coming up next week. But if you think about it all the time, you become stressed, full of tension, unable to relax, unable to feel good or study.

Put everything that is taking up space in your mind on a shelf. There's nothing you can do about it now.

and

imagine that you have a trash can under the shelf.

Think of the things you don't need to concern yourself with anymore.

Put them in the trash can.

Now, you can be free to think about the things you choose to think about. Later, when the time is right, you can take anything you want off the shelf to deal with it.

RELAXATION SYMBOL

Have the student visualize a symbol that means relaxation to them. For example, a gently soaring seagull flying high in the sky or a sail boat drifting on the distant horizon. One student I know uses a waterfall.

Visualization Exercise

Have the students close their eyes.
Now say to them:

> *Think about something that makes you feel peaceful.*
>
> *Close your eyes and let yourself picture that image.*
>
> *Now let peace and relaxation flow through your entire*
>
> *body as you keep a picture of that image in your mind.*
>
> *Feel the peace.*
>
> *Enjoy the peace.*

You can explain to them that they can keep this symbol for as long as they want, change it or vary it whenever they wish. The main point is that it will take them to a state of relaxation that works for them. Tell them:

> *Your mind will be able to picture this symbol with greater*
>
> *ease the more you use it. As your mind pictures your*
>
> *symbol, your body will begin to respond automatically by*
>
> *relaxing itself more and more quickly as you continue this*
>
> *practice. There will soon come a time when all you need*
>
> *to do is picture your symbol and your body will almost*
>
> *simultaneously become relaxed. This is a very valuable*
>
> *technique for use in all the stressful times in your life.*

The more you can visualize your symbol in your mind, the greater impression it will make on your subconscious.

CREATIVE EXERCISE

Material needed: Index cards, crayons or colored pencils, a variety of magazines, paste and scissors.

Let students pick out their own materials.

Ask them to picture their symbol in their mind and draw it as well as they can. It does not have to be perfect. Just draw the idea of their symbol or see if they can find a picture of it in a magazine. Then cut it out and paste it on their file card or on another sheet of paper.

Have them write:

My Symbol Is (One word or full description)

_____

_____

_____

_____

_____

_____

This technique works with all ages groups. You can make it a project for as long as you wish and time permits. Students can carry the card with them or put it somewhere where they will see it often. If you have access to a laminating machine, it will last longer! Whenever they see the picture, a feeling of peace will be triggered.

IMPULSE CONTROL AND DELAYED GRATIFICATION

An impulse is when we act on our feelings without thinking. It is taking actions or reactions to things you want to do without thinking it through.

When we don't stop and think:

an EVENT_____ leads to a REACTION.

Something happens and we react to it.

Instead, by simply pausing and bringing attention to their breath, students learn they have a choice. They can give their full attention to what is going on in the moment. Instead of running away from or being afraid of uncomfortable thinking or difficult emotions (with anger or addictions or violence), they learn that all their feelings are okay. It's acting out on them that can get them in trouble!

With impulse control students learn the power of a pause:

EVENT_____PAUSE_____CHOICE

Students can learn to express their feelings in a healthy way. They use the "I" message.

For example, they can say:

I am feeling ANGRY!

I feel like punching something!

I feel so angry I want to break that window!

By taking the time to pause, they can notice, observe and name their feelings, which helps put distance between the feeling and the action.

PRACTICING IMPULSE CONTROL AND DELAYED GRATIFICATION

Have your students select one activity they do on a regular basis, eating their lunch, for example. Instead of automatically taking a bite, explain that they should count 5 full breaths first. They should then notice what they are feeling. For example, if they feel silly or impatient or even angry, simply notice it. Feel what "impatience" or "silly" or "angry" feels like in their body. Maybe they'll even find themselves smiling and enjoying the exercise.

Explain that whatever they feel is neither right nor wrong. This is an exercise in learning to observe one's feelings without needing to act on them.

Older students could practice answering the telephone at home. Instead of rushing to answer the telephone, they can let it ring one more time or let the answering machine take the call. Just because a phone is ringing, there is no need to automatically run to answer it. Again, they can just notice their feelings as they alter their usual way of doing things.

Watching TV is another way students can practice delayed gratification at home. Instead of automatically turning the TV on, they can STOP! They can then count 10 full breaths before turning it on the TV. Perhaps they will feel irritable or angry that they are making themselves wait. They should simply observe their feelings.

These are excellent techniques for increasing impulse control and learning the benefits of delayed gratification. Just because someone wants something now does not mean they have to have it, now. They do not even have to have it at all if it is something unhealthy or detrimental. For example, if a student wants to hit another student, by practicing impulse control through counted breaths, he or she will learn that by waiting, the feelings have a chance to go away and be replaced with feelings of calm and patience. By taking the time to breathe in and out ten times, feelings change. The anger might still be there, but the need to do something unhealthy about it will dissipate.

This is an excellent technique to use for staying away from other unhealthy habits such as drinking, drugging, smoking, binging or starving.

RAISINS OR M&Ms

Good for practicing mindfulness, impulse control and delayed gratification

Here is another fun way of helping to get the students to be in the moment and wake up their awareness to their senses. Have a supply of either raisons or M&Ms to pass out.

Raisons are good because they have a wonderful texture and take a long time to chew. They also have a strong aroma. The downside is that there might be someone who doesn't like raisons. Ask each student to take one raison and look it over very carefully. Look at all the groves and wrinkles. Ask the class to very slowly feel all the textures with their fingers. Then ask your students to put the raison under their nose and smell it. Next, ask them to put the raison in their mouth but do not swallow or even chew it. Let it just stay in their mouths getting familiar with the taste and the texture. Resist any temptation to chew or swallow it. Ask them to notice how they react to any resistance. Drag this out as long as is reasonable and then ask them to chew it very slowly, being mindful of the juices, tastes, smells and even sounds that they experience in the process, before they finally swallow it.

You might want to do this exercise with M&Ms instead. The downside of M&M's is that some kids are allergic to chocolate. It might be helpful to have some raisins on hand for these students. The experience with M&Ms is very different. Ask them to take one M&M and look it over very carefully, very slowly feeling its surface with their fingers. Then ask them to put the M&M under their nose and smell it.

Ask the students to put one on their tongue. Ask them to resist chewing or swallowing it but just be aware as it slowly melts. Ask them to be aware of their feelings as they are mindful of this experience.

Whichever you choose to use serves well in teaching about being in the moment. It is also a wonderful lesson in reinforcing impulse control and delayed gratification!

Understandably, some students will feel very frustrated. They want to swallow it NOW and not wait. Others are fascinated by the experience and gain new awareness into their own personality, such as seeing their own impatience or really tasting an M&M or raison for the first time.

This is a good opportunity to have a discussion at the end of the exercise. Questions such as:

How did this feel when you were very slowly chewing the raisin or letting or letting the M&M melt on your tongue?

Did you enjoy it?

What did you notice about the raisin or M&M that you never realized before?

TIMES TO USE STOP! FOR PERSONAL EMPOWERMENT

There are times when stopping and bringing your focus to your breath for just one minute can change a C to a B on an exam or an upsetting mood to one of relaxation. **Practice STOP! 5 to 20 minutes every morning!** Then, when you are in a stressful situation, it will be natural for you to remember the power of your breath.

 Take one minute and quietly be with your breath:

> ★ **Before making a speech**
> ★ **Before taking a test or quiz**
> ★ **Before studying**
> ★ **When doing something new**
> ★ **When feeling uncomfortable**
> ★ **When feeling afraid or not good about yourself**
> ★ **When feeling angry**

★ STOP! when you hear the bell ring and be aware of your breath
★ STOP! 10 seconds before getting up for the next class.
★ Smile as you breathe in and feel the power of your breath coming into your body
★ Write the word STOP! on the top of your exam paper to remember to breathe and relax
★ Put a STOP! DO YOU KNOW YOU'RE BREATHING sticker on your exam paper to remember to BREATHE
★ STOP! And change your feelings with words. Think of something that makes you smile, or feel gentle or happy such as: a puppy, a lollipop, or a sunset.
★ Write the word PEACE on a piece of paper. STOP! and know that you have peace with you at all times.
★ STOP! and find the power of the pause

DAILY PRACTICE

Practice mindfulness 20 minutes each day

Be aware of your self talk, beliefs and opinions

When feeling stressed, bring your attention to your breath.

Count your breaths for one minute

Do the "Smile On Your Toes" technique

Do the "Palms Over Your Hand" technique

Say or write positive affirmations

Know that you are terrific just the way you are!

MINDFULNESS SCRIPTS

Here are three scripts: long, short, and even shorter. Choose the appropriate script ro read to your students according to the age of your students and the time available. You don't have to read these exactly as they are. They are simply to be used as a guide until you're comfortable guiding your class using your own words.

Full Long Script

This can take anywhere from 12-20 minutes.

This is the same script as found on page 14 with just a slight change in the ending.

Sit comfortably, with your back as straight as possible, your chin tucked down enough so that the back of your neck is straight. If you are sitting in a chair, have your feet uncrossed and flat on the floor. If you are sitting crossed-legged, it is okay to lean against the wall, if you wish, with your back as straight as possible.

Close your eyes very gently and begin to breathe in and breathe out.

Don't try to control your breathing in any way. Just let it be natural.

Now...

> *Let your entire body relax.*

> > *Let your breath take on its own natural rhythm.*

Feel relaxation flowing from the top of your head

> *all the way down to the bottom of your feet.*

Feel your scalp relaxing...

>your forehead...

>eyelids...

>all the muscles around your eyes.

Relax your nose...

>sinuses...

>all the bones and muscles of your face.

Relax around your jaw, where we hold a lot of tension.

Now relax your mouth...

>chin...

>down your throat.

Feel all your tension pouring down the back of your neck...

>poring down and your shoulders.

>All tension and stress, anxiety, resistance,

>all negativity

>pouring down your arms...

>into your hands and fingers...

>into the tips of your fingers

>and completely leaving your body through the tips of your

>fingers.

Now relax your chest...

>diaphragm...

>all the knots and muscles of your stomach.

And let any stress you still might have pour

down your spine...

all stress and tension, fear, negativity

feel it emptying down into the small of your back

down through your hips...

buttocks...

thighs...

down through your knees and legs...

into your ankles...

toes...

into the tips of your toes...

and completely leaving your body through the tips of your

toes.

Now go back and check your body for any left over

tightness and bring relaxation to them.

And then return your attention to your breathing

as you breathe in

and you breathe out...

as you breathe in

and you breathe out.

Know that as you breathe in,

you are breathing in powerful, positive energy.

You're breathing in peace

and breathing out tension.

And as you breath out you are exhaling.

You're letting go of everything

     that is keeping you from feeling peace.

Get to know all the characteristics of your breath.

Now sit quietly and be aware of your breathing.

Be aware of your breath

     as it goes in and as it goes out of your nose.

Just notice your breath,

     as it goes in and as it goes out.

See if you can notice if it's cool or warm,

     long or short.

Is it rough or smooth?

Don't change it. Just let it be and observe it as it is.

Notice if it's shallow or deep.

Notice if it changes.

If thoughts come in, just let them be and go back to your
breathing.

If feelings come up, just notice them and go back to your
breathing.

If you experience an itch or a pain, try not to move.

Bring your attention to that area of your body

     and watch it as it changes and moves away.

If you get lost in a thought or a daydream, just notice that you

     got lost and bring your attention back to your breathing.

It's helpful to make a mental note of what it was that took you
   away from your breathing.
Name it without judgment and then return
      to your breathing.
Know that as you are breathing in, you are continuing to fill
with powerful, healing energy.
And as you breathe out you are exhaling everything negative
      that blocks you from feeling good.
Breathing in peace...
      Breathing out tension...
Breathing in love...
      Breathing out resentments...
 Breathing in...
        breathing out...
Breathing in...
      breathing out...
Pause now to give them time to be with their breath. However
long you think they can handle from 3-5 minutes the first time.
Then say: Now get ready to come back to this room. Be sure to
count to five and very slowly open your eyes.
            Peace!

Short Script

Use when you have five or ten minutes.
Good when you have just a few minutes or to have the class get centered and relaxed right before an exam.

Sit comfortably, with your back as straight as possible, your chin tucked down enough so that the back of your neck is straight. If you are sitting in a chair, have your feet uncrossed and flat on the floor. If you are sitting crossed-legged, it is okay to lean against the wall, if you wish, with your back as straight as possible.

Close your eyes very gently and begin to breathe in and breathe out.

Don't try to control your breathing in any way. Just let it be natural.

Now... Let your entire body relax.

Let your breath take on its own natural rhythm.

Feel relaxation flowing from the top of your head all the way down to the bottom of your feet.

Feel all your stress and tension, negativity, fear, concerns, anxieties...

completely leaving your body through the tips of your fingers

and the tips of your toes.

And then return your attention to your breathing

as you breathe in

and you breathe out...

as you breathe in

and you breathe out.

Know that as you breathe in,

you are breathing in powerful, positive energy.

You're breathing in peace

and breathing out tension.

And as you breath out you are exhaling.

You're letting go of everything

that is keeping you from feeling peace.

You can say to yourself

I am breathing in, I am breathing out   or

I am breathing in peace, I am breathing out tension

When thoughts come in, just let them be and go back to your breathing.

If you get lost in a thought or a daydream, just notice that you got lost and bring your attention back to your breathing.

It's helpful to make a mental note of what it was that took you away from your breathing.

Name it without judgment and then return to your breathing.

Know that as you are breathing in, you are continuing to fill with powerful, healing energy.

And as you breathe out you are exhaling everything negative that blocks you from feeling good.

Breathing in peace...

Breathing out tension...

Breathing in love...

Breathing out resentments...

 Breathing in...

  breathing out...

Breathing in...

  breathing out...

Stay with this as long as you want and whenever you're ready, bring your attention back to your room. Be sure to count to five and very slowly open your eyes.

    Peace!

An Even Shorter Script

This is effective and can be used when you only have 2 or 3 minutes!

Sit comfortably, with your back as straight as possible, and close
your eyes.

Very gently and begin to breathe in and breathe out.

Let your breath take on its own natural rhythm.

Now let your entire body relax.

Feel relaxation flowing from the top of your head
  all the way down to the bottom of your feet.

Feel all your stress and tension, negativity, fear, concerns,
 anxieties...

Completely leaving your body
    through the tips of your fingers
      and the tips of your toes.

And then return your attention to your breathing.

Feel your breath as you breathe in
    and you breathe out...
      as you breathe in
        and you breathe out.

Know that as you breathe in,
    you are breathing in powerful, positive energy.

You're breathing in peace
    and breathing out tension.

And as you breath out you are exhaling.

You're letting go of everything

that is keeping you from feeling relaxation and peace.

You can say to yourself

I am breathing in, I am breathing out or

I am breathing in peace,

I am breathing out tension

When thoughts come in, just let them be and go back to your

breathing.

Know that as you are breathing in, you are continuing to fill

with powerful, healing energy.

And as you breathe out you are exhaling everything negative

that blocks you from feeling realxed.

Breathing in peace...Breathing out tension...

Breathing in...breathing out...

Breathing in...breathing out...

Now...bring your attention back to your room. Be sure to count

to five and very slowly open your eyes.

Peace!

STOP! BOOKLET

On the following page you will see a simple script that students can keep with them and practice whenever they wish. It is very simple, ideal for younger students, but can be used with older students as well.

It is designed so that when folded, it becomes a little booklet.
1. Photocopy as many sheets as you need.
2. Take each sheet and fold it in half.
3. Fold in half again.

Do you know your breath is like a
miracle?
You just have to

STOP

to know it's there!
STOP!
Now!
And now breathe!
Can you feel it?
Do you notice it?
You will feel it if you
STOP
Be aware of your breath now.
Do nothing else but notice it.
Notice it as it
goes in and goes out.
Now count each breath as they go in
and go out.
It's a simple as
1, 2, 3

See how simple it is to count each
time you breathe in and out?
Do you know that we breathe on the
average of 30 times a minute?
Do you know that we breathe on the
average of 40,000 times a day?
That's a lot of breathing!
And it happens without us doing
anything at all.
It happens without us even noticing
our breathing.
We just breathe in and breathe out.
All the time. It's there.
Our breath is always there.
All we have to do is notice it,
watch it,
and follow it.
Our breath is always there,
for feeling good,
for peace
and for calm.

You can say these words as you are
breathing…
I am breathing in one.
I am breathing out one.
I am breathing in two.
I am breathing out two…
until you feel calm.
Do this for as much time as it takes
to feel calm.
I am breathing in three…
I am breathing out three…
and then,
if you forget to count
just start again at the beginning!
You can't do it wrong!
Just start right over…
as many times as you want…
I am breathing in one.
I am breathing out one.
I am breathing in two.
I am breathing out two…
and on and on and on…

DO YOU KNOW YOU'RE BREATHING?

by
Ruth Fishel

May your lives be rich and full
of the joy
and deep satisfaction
of knowing you are doing important work.

FOOT NOTES

1. Bettina Seipp, " Anxiety and Acandemic Perfermance: A Meta-analysis," Anxiety Research 4, 1 (1991)
As quoted in Emotional Intelligence by Daniel Goleman

2. Richard Metzger, "Worry Changes Decision-making: The Effects of Negative Thoughts on Cognitive Processing," Journal of Clinical Psychology (Jan.1990), As quoted in Emotional Intelligence by Daniel Goleman

Appendix

Training Customized for your School

A simple program has been established to introduce **STOP!** into your school. We can send you a trainer to create this program to fit your specific needs. Using our easy to follow program guide, the **STOP!** program can be taught by teachers to students in one hour a week sessions over a one month period. Follow-up and support sessions are designed to take place after that, with continued support made available as needed.

Once learned, **STOP!** can be practiced in only a few minutes a day, in or out of class, thereby becoming an essential tool for use in achieving ongoing improvement in the participants' lives.

A **bonus** is that because it comes complete with this easy to follow text, the program can be learned by other teachers with no additional outlay of money, thus insuring an ongoing change in the over all climate of the school.

Call us at 508-420-5301 for further information.

STOP! OFFERS RESULTS

THIS IS A PARTIAL LIST OF SCHOOLS AND BUSINESSES WHERE STOP! DO YOU KNOW YOU'RE BREATHING? HAS BEEN PRESENTED

Adcare Hospital of Worcester

American Cancer Society

American Suicide Foundation

Barnstable High School

Bourne Schools

Cape Cod Human Services

Cape Cod Technical High School

Cotuit/Marstons Mills Schools

Dennis/Yarmouth Highschool

Dighton/Rehobeth Schools

Dover Sherborn High School

Framingham Schools

Harvard Pilgrim Health Care

Harwich Schools

Marstons Mills Middle School

Mass Correctional Inst.of Framingham

Mass Dept. of Public Health Conference

New Hope Rape Crisis Center

Plymouth Elementary Schools

Quashnet Valley School

Riverview School

Roxbury Latin

Southwick Hospital

LETTERS FROM INMATES

At one time I taught a variation of **STOP!** to women at the Barnstable House of Corrections. When an inmate heard that I was beginning to teach the program in schools, she wanted students to know how much STOP! DO YOU KNOW YOU'RE BREATHING? meant to her. The following was typed from the handwritten letter she wrote to me in 1996. Her name has been changed to protect her identity.

MY name is Jane. I am in jail. I am afraid, frightened and really feeling helpless. I have been drinking most of my life. I know it is legal. But it is not legal to drink and drive.

That is what I did. I did not have an accident. However I have served almost 2 months and I can't even begin to tell you what a nightmare this is, handcuffs, shame, everything was taken. What a nightmare. What's really terrible is the TORTURE and the EMBARRASSMENT I have put my children through. I can look back now but they're the ones suffering.

This is all because I picked up a drink. Oh, don't get me wrong. I don't hang out, don't go to the bars, never did drugs, but here I sit. I am the woman who may have taught you CCD, or maybe I nursed someone in your family back to health. Oh, yes, I was at all your Little League games, basketball, and was the Mom who has everyone over for great sleep-overs. The difference between you and me is that I picked up and I am behind bars.

I have court soon and I could be here a lot longer. I just don't know. When I came into jail I was told to go to a mindfulness class called STOP! DO YOU KNOW YOU'RE BREATHING? I am a skeptic but I went for it and have now been to many classes. I believe that if I'd had I had this program in high school I would not be sitting where I am today. Instead I would be home helping my children adjust to their new school year. Mindfulness puts me into another place, a good place, and you can feel the same. Please give it a chance and see what it does for you. I swear you won't believe it. And, maybe, just maybe, you won't pick up and you won't be like I am now-LOCKED UP AND IN JAIL, not knowing where my children are.

Here is another letter from a 31 year old inmate at the Barnstable House of Corrections

To All High School Students

If I had STOP! when I was in school, I believe I would have been able to release my anger and give me some relaxation. STOP! helps you feel a sense of peace. It can put you into a place where you feel and hear nothing that is happening for a short time. This special technique puts you in full control of yourself. You can release muscular tension as well as bring your entire body into a greater balance. When you begin to relax, you can look into other ways of dealing with stressful situations. I would suggest this to any high school student because I feel if I had this in high school, it would have made a big difference in my life. My anger has been one of the reasons why I've gotten into so much trouble most of my life and is also one of the reasons why I am in jail today. Please don't let such a good opportunity go by.

Books by Ruth Fishel

HANG IN 'TIL THE MIRACLE HAPPENS
PRECIOUS SOLITUDE
THE JOURNEY WITHIN: A Spiritual Path to Recovery
TIME FOR JOY,.daily meditation and affirmations *which has sold over 300,000 copies*
TIME FOR JOY Daily Journal
TIME FOR THOUGHTFULNESS
TAKE TIME FOR YOURSELF
5 MINUTES FOR WORLD PEACE...FOREVER
CAPE COD MEMORIES
NEWPORT MEMORIES
MEMORIES OF THE FLORIDA COAST

AUDIOTAPES
TIME FOR JOY
YOU CAN'T MEDITATE WRONG
TRANSFORMING YOUR PAST INTO PRESENTS
GUIDED EXERCISES FOR DEEPENING YOUR MEDITATION EXPERIENCE
THE JOURNEY WITHIN
DISCOVERING YOUR SOURCE OF PEACE

Spirithaven

17 Pond Meadow Dr
Marstons Mills, MA 02648
Email:Spirithaven @spirithaven.com
508-420-5301

Name _____

Address _____

City, State,Zip _____

Daytime Tel and Email _____

QTY	TITLE	PRICE	TOTAL
	BOOKS		
	HANG IN 'TIL THE MIRACLE HAPPENS	$7.95	
	PRECIOUS SOLITUDE	$10.95	
	STOP! DO YOU KNOW YOU'RE BREATHING for kids	$3.50	
	STOP! DO YOU KNOW YOU'RE BREATHING? Teachers Guide	$13.95	
	TIME FOR JOY	$6.95	
	TIME FOR THOUGHTFULNESS	$7.95	
	THE JOURNEY WITHIN:A Spiritual Path to Recovery	$8.95	
	TAKE TIME FOR YOURSELF	$8.95	
	TAPES		
	YOU CAN'T MEDITATE WRONG	$10.00	
	THE JOURNEY WITHIN	$10.00	
	Discovering Your Source of Peace	$10.00	
	Guided Exercises for Deepening Your Meditation Experience	$10.00	
	Time for Joy!	$10.00	
	Transforming Your Pasts Into Presents	$10.00	
	Recovering from the Basics of Addiction	$10.00	
	STOP SMOKING! Through Self-Hypnosis	$10.00	
	Total Order		
	Shipping		
	Enclosed is my check for		

PLEASE ADD $3.50 FOR SHIPPING AND HANDLING FOR THE FIRST $25.00, PLUS $3.50 FOR THE NEXT $25.00 and 5% SALES TAX IN MASS.
Thank you for your order.